ALWAYS IN MY HEART

Written By

Jamie Stafford & Shari Stafford And
Cheryl Bayer

Illustrated By Sara Noelle Delgado

Augmented reality popups featuring the voices of:
Lily Lulu Weitzman
Karp Sal Brady

Produced and Published by Living Popups, Inc.:

Cheryl Bayer	Sara Delgado	Isaac Middleton
Thomas Bergstig	Jamie Dixon	Ken Pellegrino
Aaron Booker	Courtney Matash	Nigel Rodriguez
Nicholas Cerofeci		Erwin Umali

- Get the app -
Search **LP Bookspace** on iOS and Android

Copyright ©2023 Living Popups, Inc.

Welcome

Welcome to the Living Popups illustrated and augmented reality enabled printing of **Always in my Heart**, written by Jamie Stafford and her mother Shari Stafford along with Cheryl Bayer and illustrated by Sara Noelle Delgado.

Always in my Heart is a personal story of love, loss, understanding grief and a granddaughter's journey towards healing through finding her sign along the way.

The augmented reality companion features Lily and Karp jumping up from the pages and discussing what's happening along the way to help the reader with comprehension and to gain a better understanding of the story.

Simply start the app*, select **Always in my Heart** and when you see a teal heart behind the page number, point the camera at the illustrations and let the characters take it from there!

*Search the app-stores for
LP Bookspace

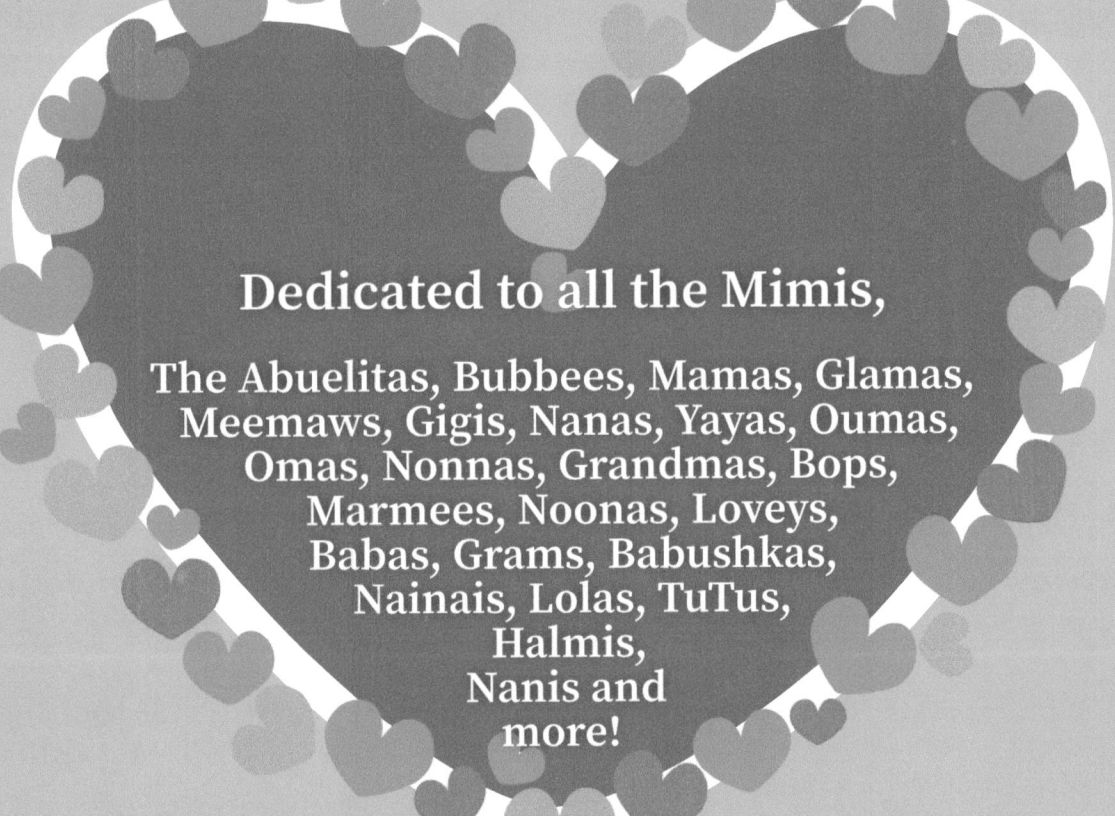

Dedicated to all the Mimis,

The Abuelitas, Bubbees, Mamas, Glamas, Meemaws, Gigis, Nanas, Yayas, Oumas, Omas, Nonnas, Grandmas, Bops, Marmees, Noonas, Loveys, Babas, Grams, Babushkas, Nainais, Lolas, TuTus, Halmis, Nanis and more!

_____

Put name here

My Grandma Mimi and I are like "two peas," they say.

We do everything together!

We love sharing popcorn at the movies, shopping for sales at the mall, and playing dress up in her humongous closet. Her high heels don't fit me just yet, but they will someday! Sometimes when I stay over at her house, she'll let me have ice cream before dinner.

I know, I'm pretty lucky.

She used to take me to school in the mornings too. All my friends know her by her flashy car and big jewelry.

But my favorite thing about my Mimi? She spent her life traveling the world. Sometimes even alone!

"I want to be just like you, Mimi," I'd tell her, "Having an adventure every- where you go!"

"And you will! Because you're my granddaughter, you're brave like me," Mimi winked.

But Mimi hasn't been herself lately.

She moved to a different place, one where lots of other Grandmas and Grandpas live. And if I'm being honest? I don't like that place too much. It's way too quiet and it smells funny.

There's something else too - she forgets things, a lot of them. Sometimes she even forgets my name, and I'm her best friend!

It makes me really sad.

"How can she forget me?" I ask mom.

With a warm smile and sad eyes, Mom would answer, "Mimi still loves you very much. She is sick right now, and that can sometimes happen when a person gets old."

Whenever I'm sick, I get better after a few days or even weeks! ...
But I guess it's different when you get old.

One day, my parents surprised me by picking me up from school early. My friends looked at me with jealous looks on their faces, but deep down inside I could tell this wasn't a "happy surprise." And, boy, was I right.

We drove to the beach, one of our favorite places to go. Usually we would be laughing and listening to songs on the radio when we drove there, but this time Mom looked like she had been crying. Dad wasn't wearing his big smile like he always does. The silence in the car felt so...strange. I had to say something.

"Why are we here?" I asked.

"We have something to tell you, and we thought we could go on a nice walk while we do," Dad said.

"Are you guys getting a divorce?" I blurted out,

"Are we moving? Wait a minute - am I finally getting a baby sister?"

I tend to ramble when I get nervous. My mother looked down at me and shook her head in a way that told me it was none of those things.

For a while we walked on the beach, listening to nothing but the waves crashing. Mom finally spoke.

With a tear rolling down her cheek, she told me something I'll never forget:

They told me Mimi had died.

At first I didn't understand,

"She's gone?" I asked, I couldn't make sense of this. Was it because I forgot to do my chores last week? Or because I didn't eat all my vegetables for dinner?

"Is it my fault?" I asked.

"Oh no, of course not!" Mom suddenly stopped walking and crouched next to me, "Everything in this world that is born will die someday, Lily. It was just Mimi's time."

Did she think this was making me feel better? Because it was totally not.

Mom continued, "but you want to know something that never dies? Love. Love never dies. Love and memories keep Mimi alive,"

Mom raised her hand and put it over my heart and softly spoke,

"Alive, but in our hearts. As long as you love your Mimi and keep her in your heart, she will always be with you."

The next thing I knew, my head was in my hands,

my face was all wet, and I just cried.

Mom and Dad cried too. I've never seen Dad cry before today. I hate that we are all so sad, but at least we're sad together.

Then it hit me, what about the last few times I saw her?

She didn't even remember who I was!

After everything we've done together, she couldn't even remember my name. This sent me over the edge, I was full blown ugly-crying.

"But what if she forgot about me, Mom?!"

Mom let out a little laugh and wiped away my tears, "Of course Mimi didn't forget you!"

"But how will I know? The last time I saw her, she looked at me like I was some stranger!"

"Oh, you'll know," Mom winked.

We all began to walk back to the car,

"Don't forget your frog!" Dad reminds me. I run back to grab it and notice something in the sand underneath it. It was a shell. It had two curved edges at the top, and a sharp point at the bottom, a perfect heart!

"Mom! Dad! Come look!" I shout, "It's a shell that looks like a heart." I held it up high for them to see.

"You know what that is, Lily?" Mom said, "...It's your sign. A sign from your Mimi. Telling you she loves you, and everything is going to be okay."

I felt myself smile once again.

The heart gave me such a good feeling, despite the bigger, bad one -

like I wasn't so alone anymore.

I tuck the shell deep inside my pocket and thought, "I guess that's what adults mean when they say Mimi will always be with me."

The next morning, I'm in bed and my mother is yelling.

I'm late for breakfast once again. Typical.

"LILY!" I hear again from downstairs. How can she expect me to pull myself out of my warm comfy blankets? She yells again, "Lily, downstairs NOW!" Alright already, I thought to myself.

::sniff sniff::

She's yelling. I'm smelling.

"Lily! I made your favorite, biscuits!"

The woman knows me too well.

I leap out of bed, change out of my pajamas, and rush to the table.

It wasn't until my first bite that I remembered the news from yesterday. It knocked all the wind out of my sails.

There I was, chowing down, it wasn't until I took my last bite that something on my plate caught my eye. A tiny crumb from the biscuit was staring back at me. Like the shell I found on the beach, it was also in the shape of a perfect heart! I couldn't contain myself.

"Mom! Dad! It happened again!" I shouted. "What happened again?" Dad asked

"Another heart! Another sign from Mimi!"

"That's awesome, sweetheart! Since you can't save it, let's just take a picture of it for you,"

Dad took out his phone and snapped the picture. Once he prints it,

I will put it right next to the heart shell.

Being at school again felt different. I don't feel brave or strong, like Mimi always was. Some of my classmates asked why I got to leave early yesterday. I just felt uncomfortable, like I wasn't ready to talk about Mimi without my tears from getting all over everything!

Would I ever get to talk about Mimi again?

During recess, Karp, my best friend wanted to play on the playground. We did this everyday, so I knew it was coming. I just didn't feel up to it. The memory of Mimi kept coming at me in waves, and, well, I just felt sad,

"You wanna go play on the monkey bars?" Karp asked. "No. Not today," I shrugged.

I turned around and walked away before I could see Karp's reaction.

I'm sure he was sad, but so was I! I guess I'll just go sit on the bench next to Mr. Cooper.

"What's wrong, Lily? Did you and Karp get into a fight?" Mr. Cooper asked.

"No. I just don't feel like playing right now." I replied, kicking the rocks under my feet.

"Would you like to talk about it?"

I was so glad Mr. Cooper asked me this, he always knew what to say.

"You remember my Grandma Mimi?" I asked. "Yes, I do," Mr. Cooper said.

"Well...she--she died yesterday," I let out.

It took everything not to cry all over the bench we were sitting on. I couldn't let him see me cry!

"I'm sorry to hear that, Lily, she was a really nice lady," Mr. Cooper told me. Then he asked me something that totally changed how sad I was feeling, "Tell me about her."

I couldn't help smiling from ear to ear because all my favorite memories came rushing back to me. I told him about her traveling stories, playing dress up, and all the ice cream cones we shared together.

I even told him about the hearts I had been finding.

"The hearts make me feel better," I told him, "My mom says that they are signs that Mimi loves me and that everything is going to be okay."

Mr. Cooper sat there for a while in silence and finally turned to me. He took a long breath in and then spoke.

"I had a wife once. Years ago, but she got very sick and passed away. We had a song, our song, that we danced to at our wedding. And you know, Lily, every time I feel sad and miss her, I play that song. I play it loud and start dancing to it. It almost feels like she's with me again."

"Just like my hearts!" I shouted.

Mr. Cooper laughed at my outburst, "Yes, Lily, just like your hearts.

The song reminds me of my love for her and makes me know that everything is going to be okay. But that's why memories are so important, you know.

In the end, all of us will be nothing but a memory."

"Might as well make it a good one!" I said.

After school, Karp and I walked home together.

Our walks remind me of the times Mimi used to pick us up and drive us home. Days like today, I really missed those times.

But, I must admit that the path Karp and I take home has quickly become one of my favorite parts of the day.

We go under big green trees that form a tunnel in the road. I'm sure Karp knows something is up! I'm usually never this quiet, but I really just don't know what to say.

"So...what did you and Mr. Cooper talk about today during recess?" Karp asked.

"Well...ugh, my Mimi died, so we talked about her mostly."

"Oh," Karp said surprised, "I'm-I'm so sorry, Lily. I really liked Mimi."

"Yeah..." I said, "You know when somebody dies and people say stuff like, 'they'll always be with you'?"

Karp nodded.

"Well that's what Mr. Cooper and I were talking about. How we have signs from the person, or even our pets, that we have loved and died. Whenever we see those signs out in the world, it's a reminder that they love us and they're always with us in our hearts. Mr. Cooper still plays a song for his wife who died a long time ago, and my signs are the hearts that I find."

"Hearts?" Karp questioned.

"Yes, hearts. I found a shell on the beach that looks like a perfect heart and there was a crumb heart on my breakfast plate this morning. Seeing them makes me feel a lot happier."

I could tell Karp was happy to see me smiling again.

"I know what you mean," Karp assures. "You do?" I smiled.

"Yes. My Dad has been gone from us for a long time. The last time I saw him I was just a baby, but he left me a box of all his things. It had a guitar, guitar picks, and some music that he wrote. I still haven't been able to play all of his songs yet, but I try to. I practice them a lot. When I play on his guitar I feel closer to him somehow. Does that make sense?"

"Totally," I said, "Signs can be from anything, just like Mr. Cooper said, the guitar picks are your sign."

We arrived at Karp's house and as he walked up his cobblestone driveway to get to his front door, he suddenly stopped.

"Lily!" He shouted, "Lily you're never going to believe!"

He grabs something off the ground and comes running back to me, full speed.

"A heart! It's a heart!" He waves the rock up in the air

and then hands it to me, "Is this what you're talking about?"

"Oh wow, Karp, it really is a heart! See? It's a sign!" I yell.

I give him a big hug as he hands it to me.

Another one to add to my collection!

Over time, I collected so many different heart-shaped things.

Mom was right though, there wasn't a sign from Mimi everyday, but I got pretty good at spotting them all around me. They would come from the most unexpected places. Some were big, waaay too big for me to keep. Some were small, waaay too small for me to hold, but the ones that I could fit into my pocket I kept and put inside a box I hid under my bed.

My friends and family even got in on it.

At recess, my friend Brooke came up to me holding a heart shaped wood chip she found underneath the playground.

My Aunt surprised me with a heart shaped stone she found in her backyard.

Everyone was on the quest of spotting my sign and sharing them with me.

It seemed as if Mimi's memory was everywhere! It made me feel so good inside.

I became The Heart Girl.

Before I knew it, the box that hid all my heart treasures was full! Every heart I collected had a story behind it, like the travels my Mimi used to tell me about. I felt more close to her than ever. It was still hard though, sometimes. I really did miss seeing Mimi and doing all the fun things like we used to.

But whenever I feel sad, I would go to my room, feel around underneath my bed, and pull out the box that had all my hearts inside. Once I open it and look at all my treasures, it feels like a hug I used to get from Mimi. In those moments, I feel Mimi is really with me giving me the courage and bravery to be happy again.

Where I once felt alone and lost without Mimi, now there is comfort and love.

My box of hearts will always remind me that my Mimi loves me and she will be...

Always In My Heart.

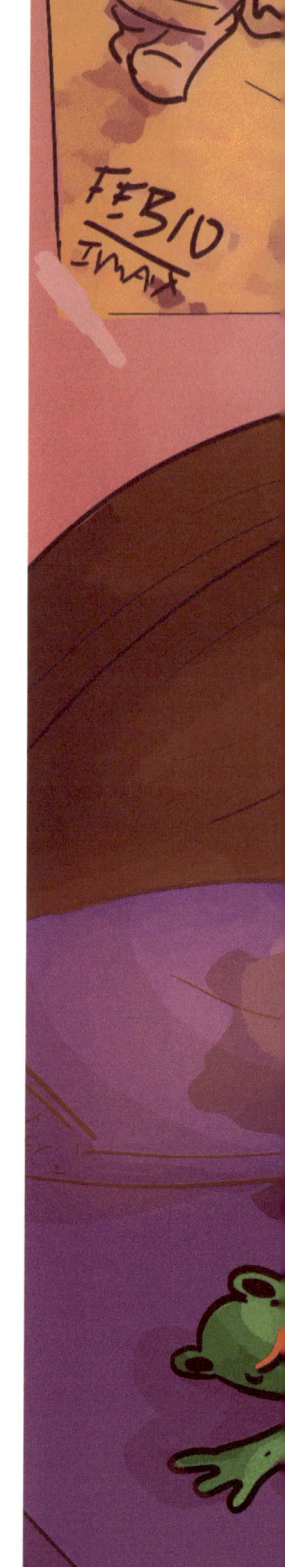

Do you have someone special in your life who has died? Who are they and why are they special to you?

Tell me your favorite memory with them!

Every time you see

_____,

you will know that is your sign that

_____

loves you and will always be in your heart.

Can you find all of my heart signs I've collected?

A portion of the proceeds of every book sold go to support

OUR HOUSE GRIEF SUPPORT CENTER.

If you are struggling with loss, reach out. You're not alone and there are people who will listen.

It all started when my little girl, Jamie handed me my first heart shaped rock and said " I love you, Mommy. Think of me". I replied "I love you too, always in my heart". And so it began, a lifetime of hearts. Finding little heart shaped rocks became, between the two of us, our sign of security, comfort and of course – Love. As Jamie grew older, the heart exchanges became less frequent. By then however, my Mother and I took to spotting our own hearts for each other. This continued until I found myself paying visits to her, suffering from Alzheimer's. As she grew older, the heart exchange also grew less.

Their impact however, remained as sturdy as… well, a rock.

I will never forget the morning after my Mother passed, feeling a loneliness so deep that all I could do was look up to the clouds. The cloud above was shaped like a perfect heart. I felt overwhelming comfort having her near. I wasn't alone anymore.

Like my Mother before me, and my daughter before that- the hearts are still our sign of security, comfort and love. They always seem to show up when I need them the most.

I wrote this story to help children cope with loss, whether a family member, friend, pet or others. Hoping the comfort I get from these signs brings the same comfort to them.

- Shari Stafford

Paste Photo Here!

Thank you for enjoying

Always In My Heart

in augmented reality!

Look for more titles at:

livingpopups.com

For a heart location key, check
livingpopups.com/always-hearts

*"I'll wait until
it comes out in AR!"*

Living Popups